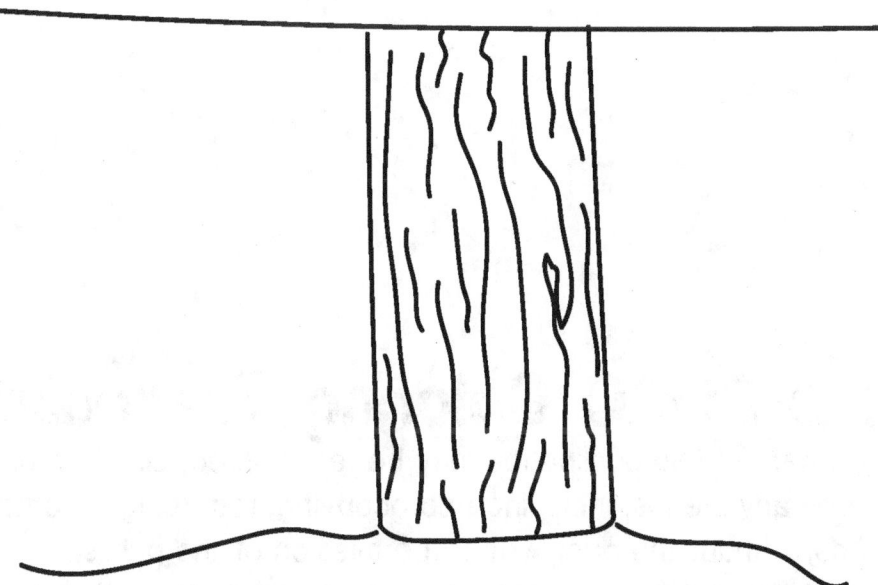

This Coloring Book Belongs To:

_____

Copyright © 2020 Coloring Tranquility

All rights reserved. No part of this publication may be reproduced, distributed, or transmitted in any form or by any means, including photocopying, recording, or other electronic or mechanical methods, without the prior written permission of the publisher, except in the case of brief quotations embodied in critical reviews and certain other noncommercial uses permitted by copyright law.

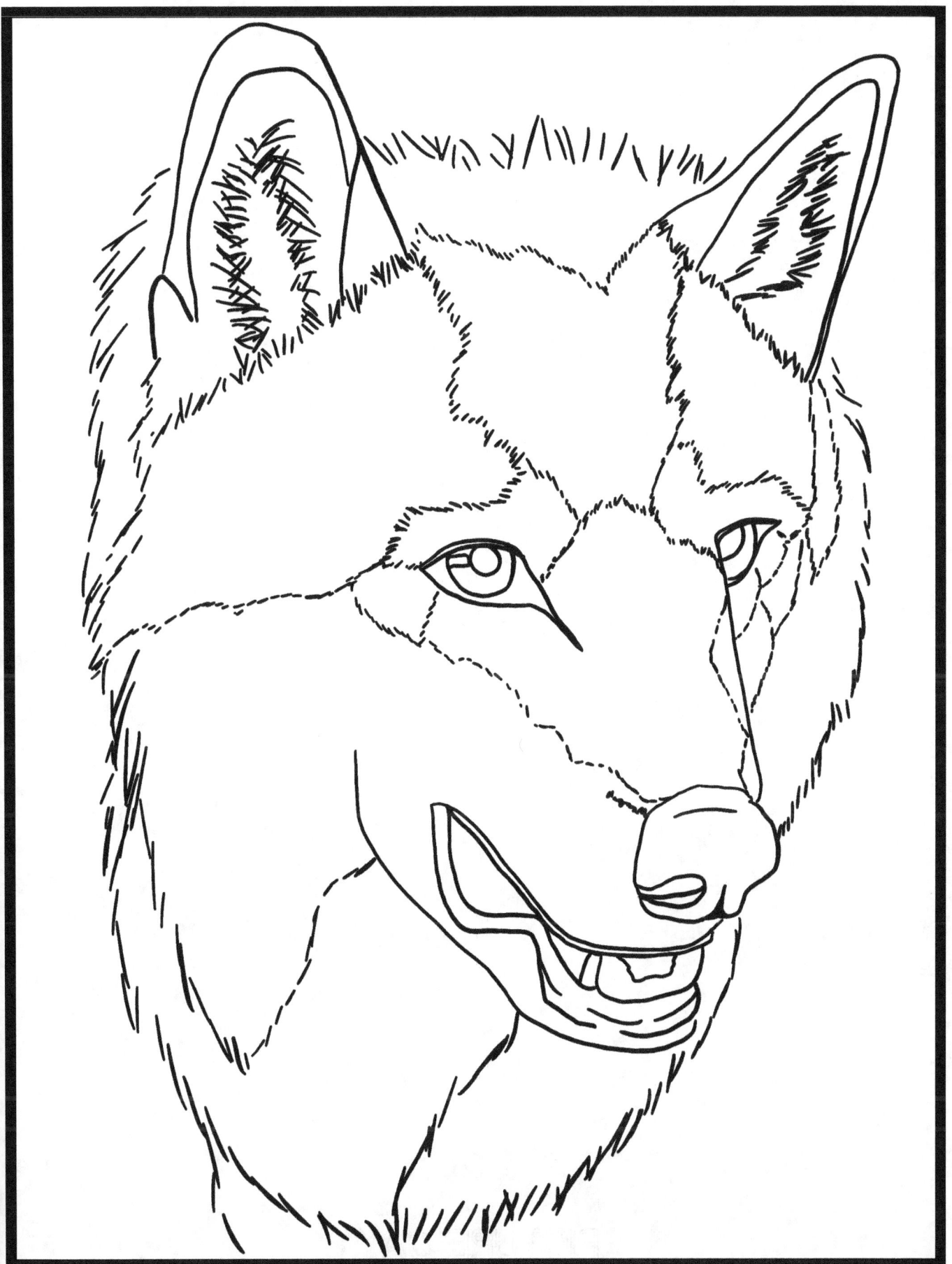

PICTURE DAY

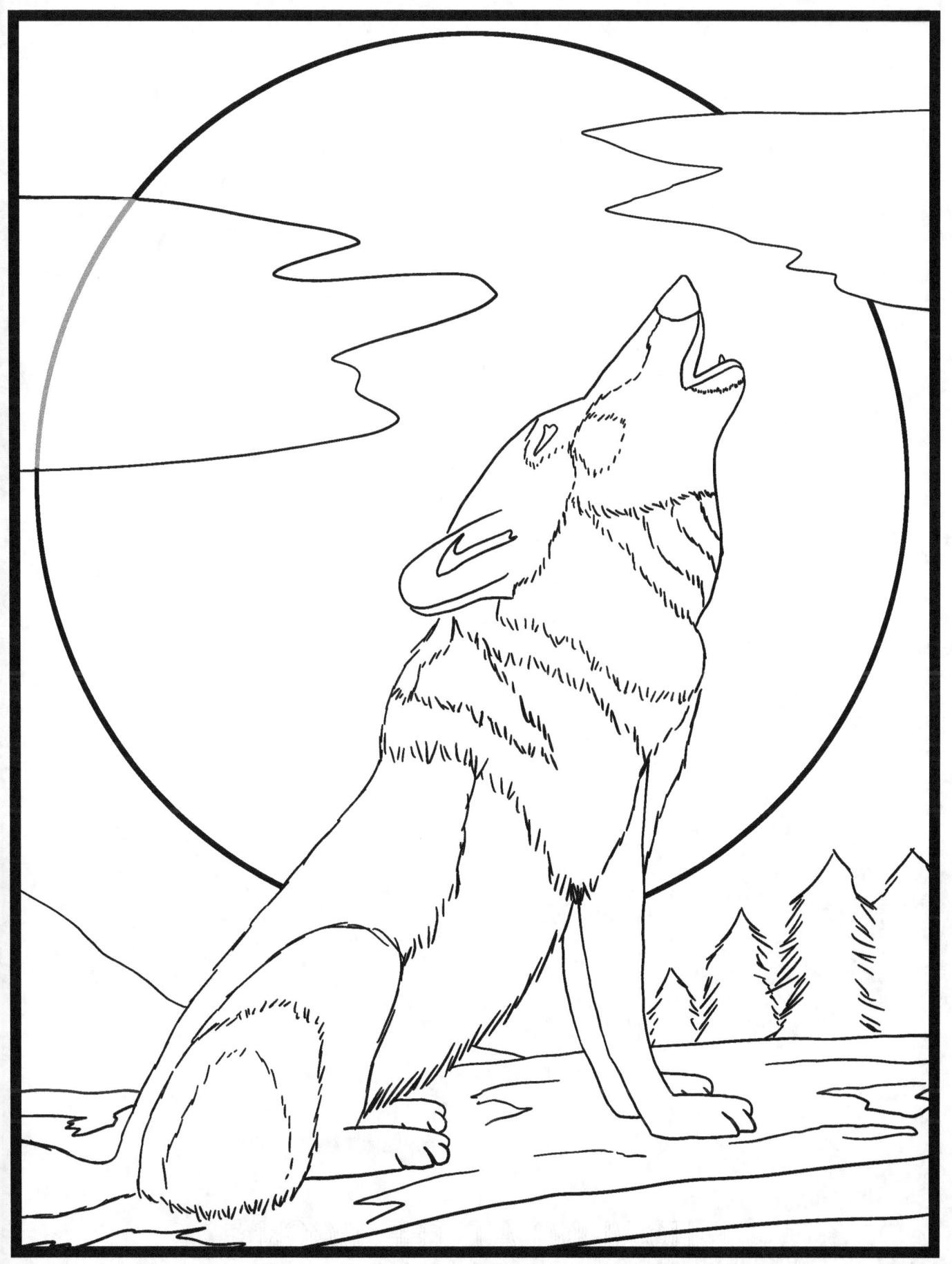

HOWLING AT THE MOON

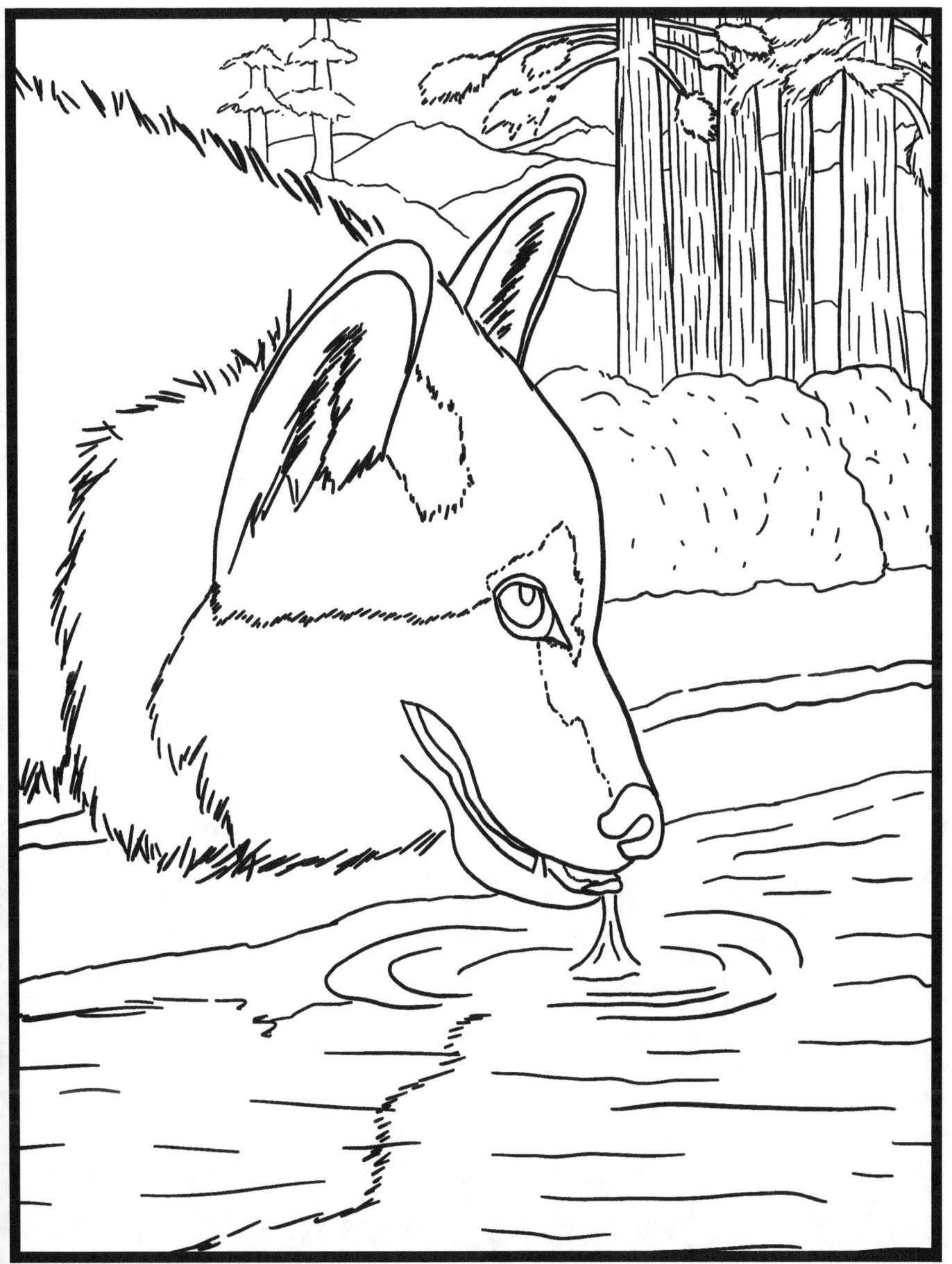

COOL DRINK OF WATER

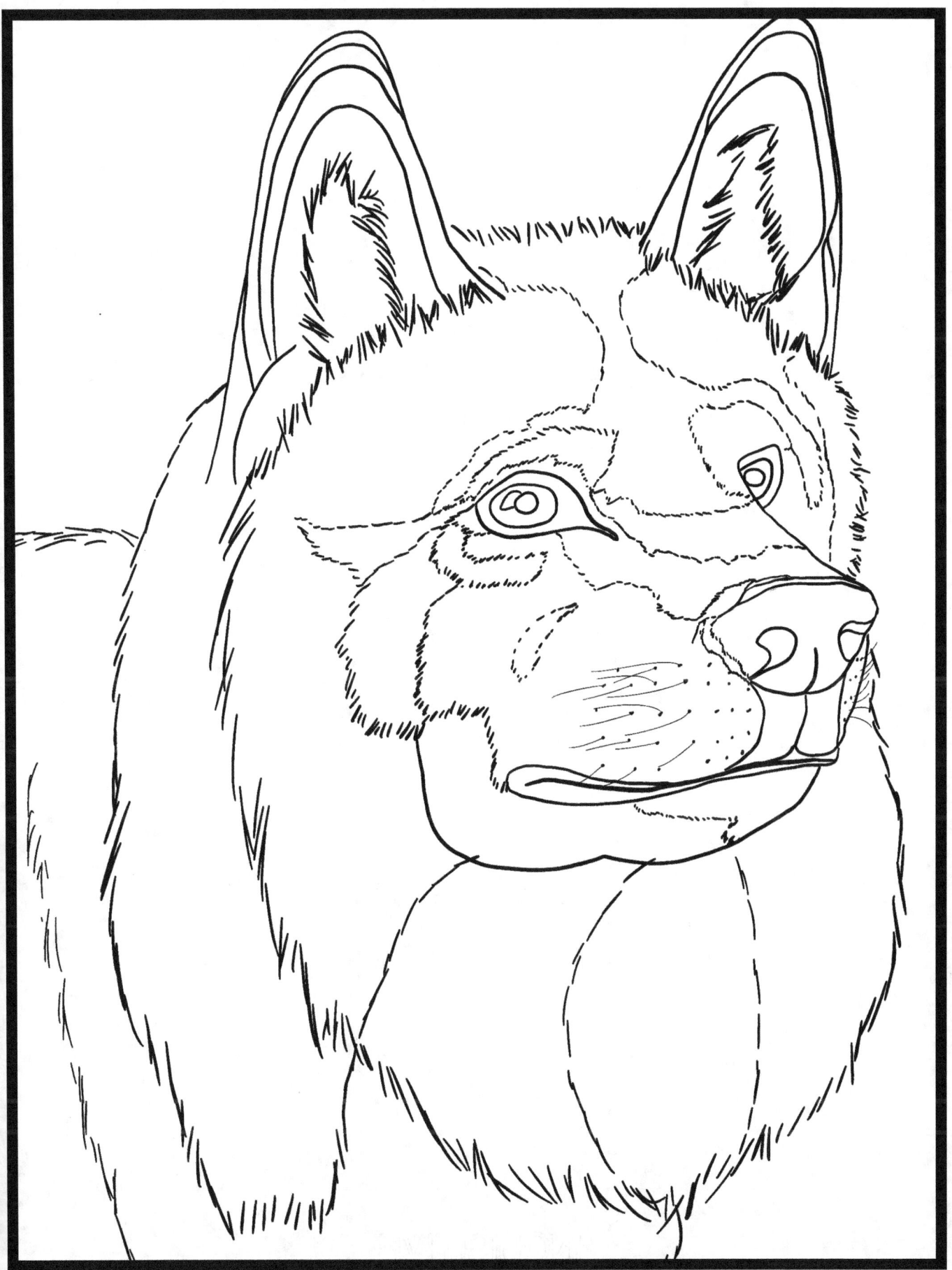

INQUISITIVE

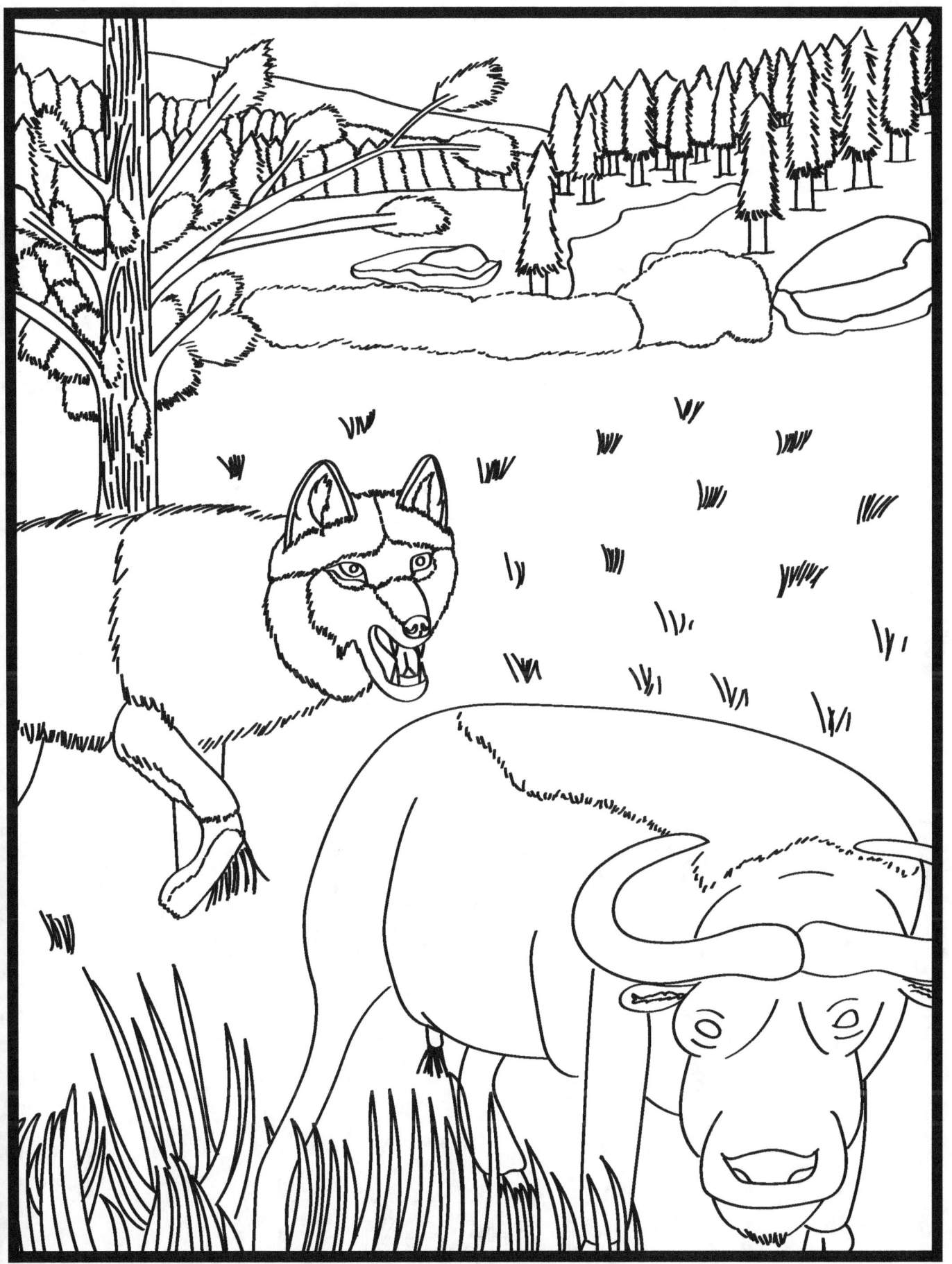

ON THE HUNT

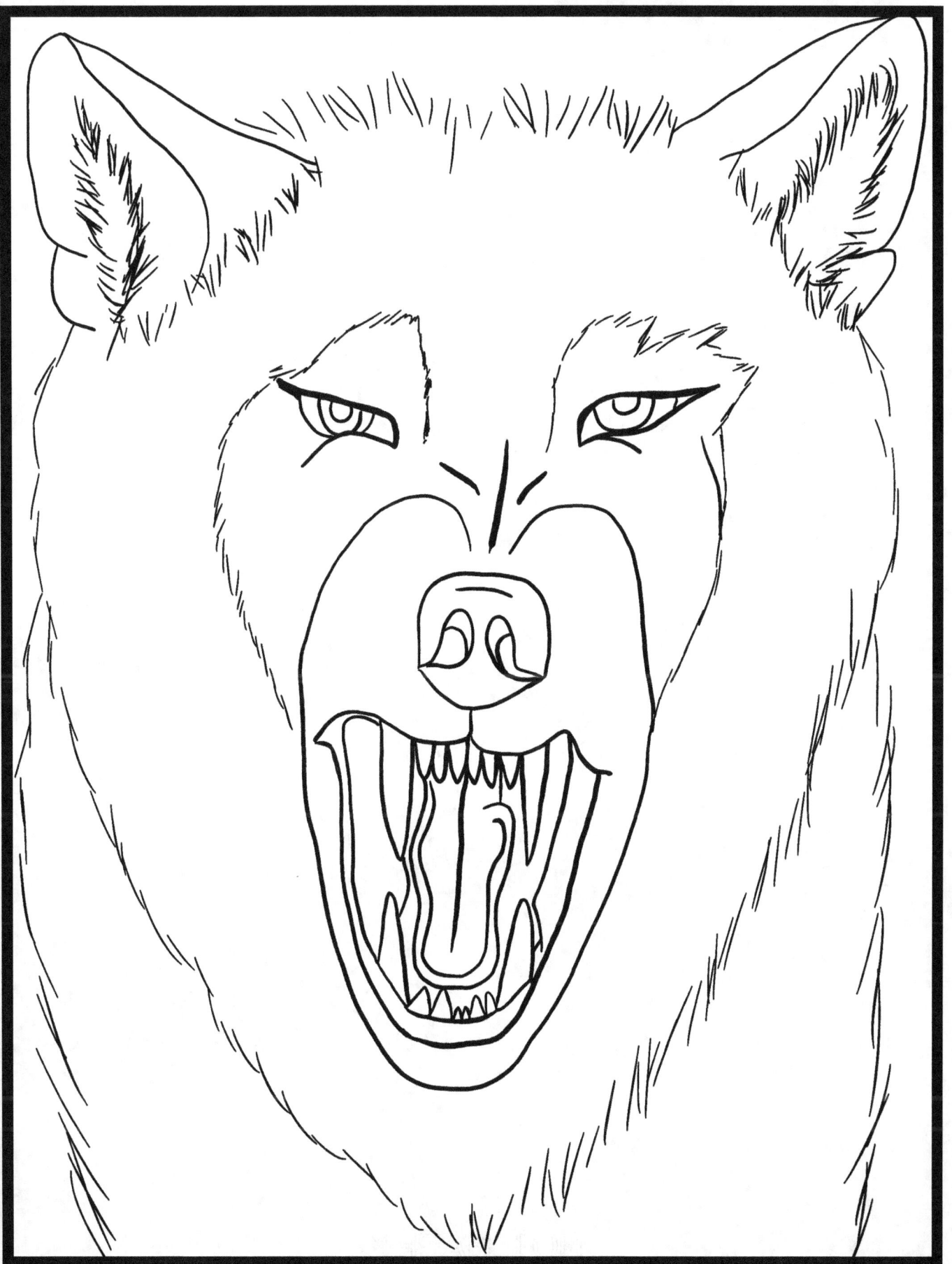

NOT HAPPY

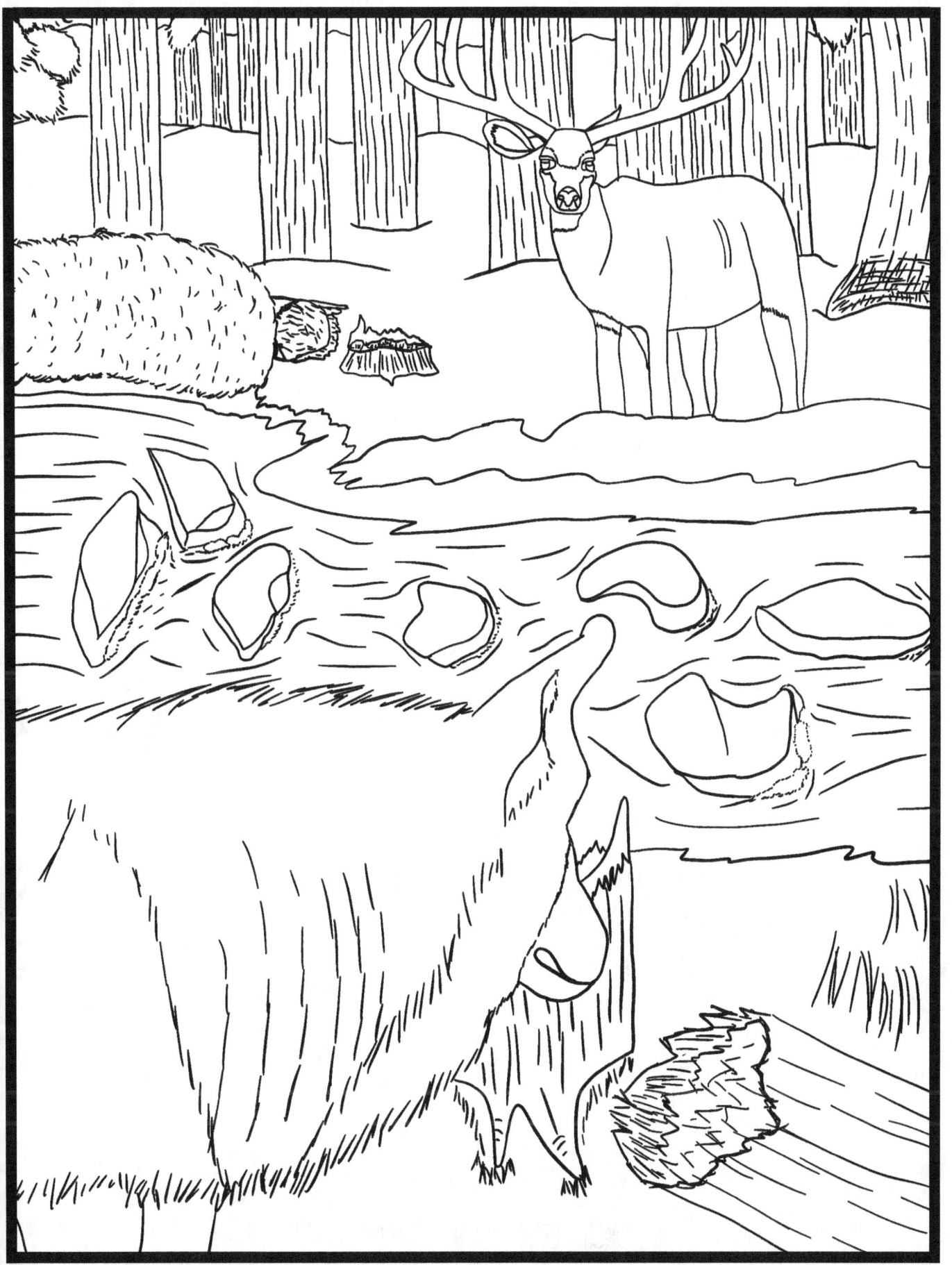

LOCKED ON TARGET

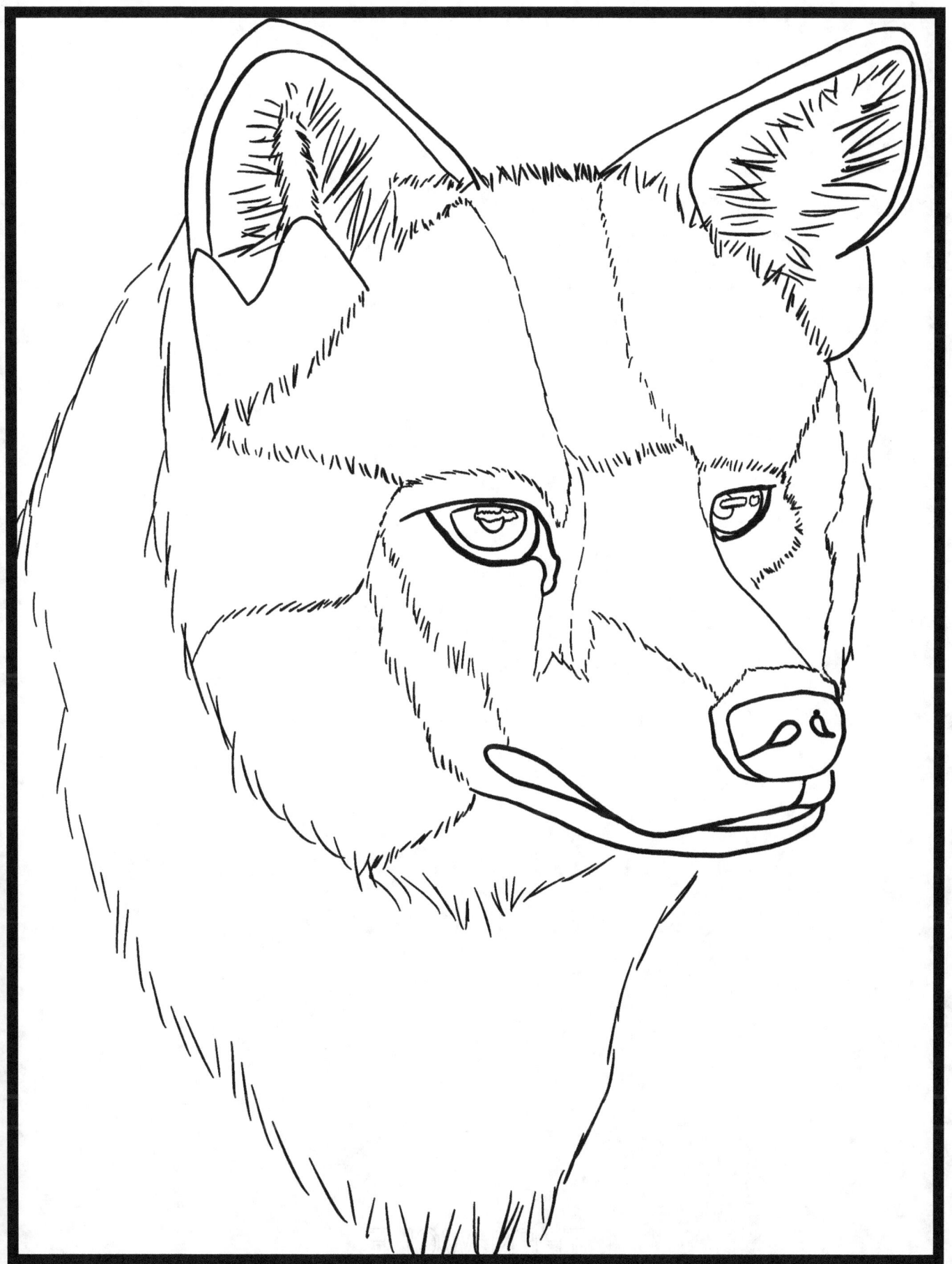

TEEN WOLF

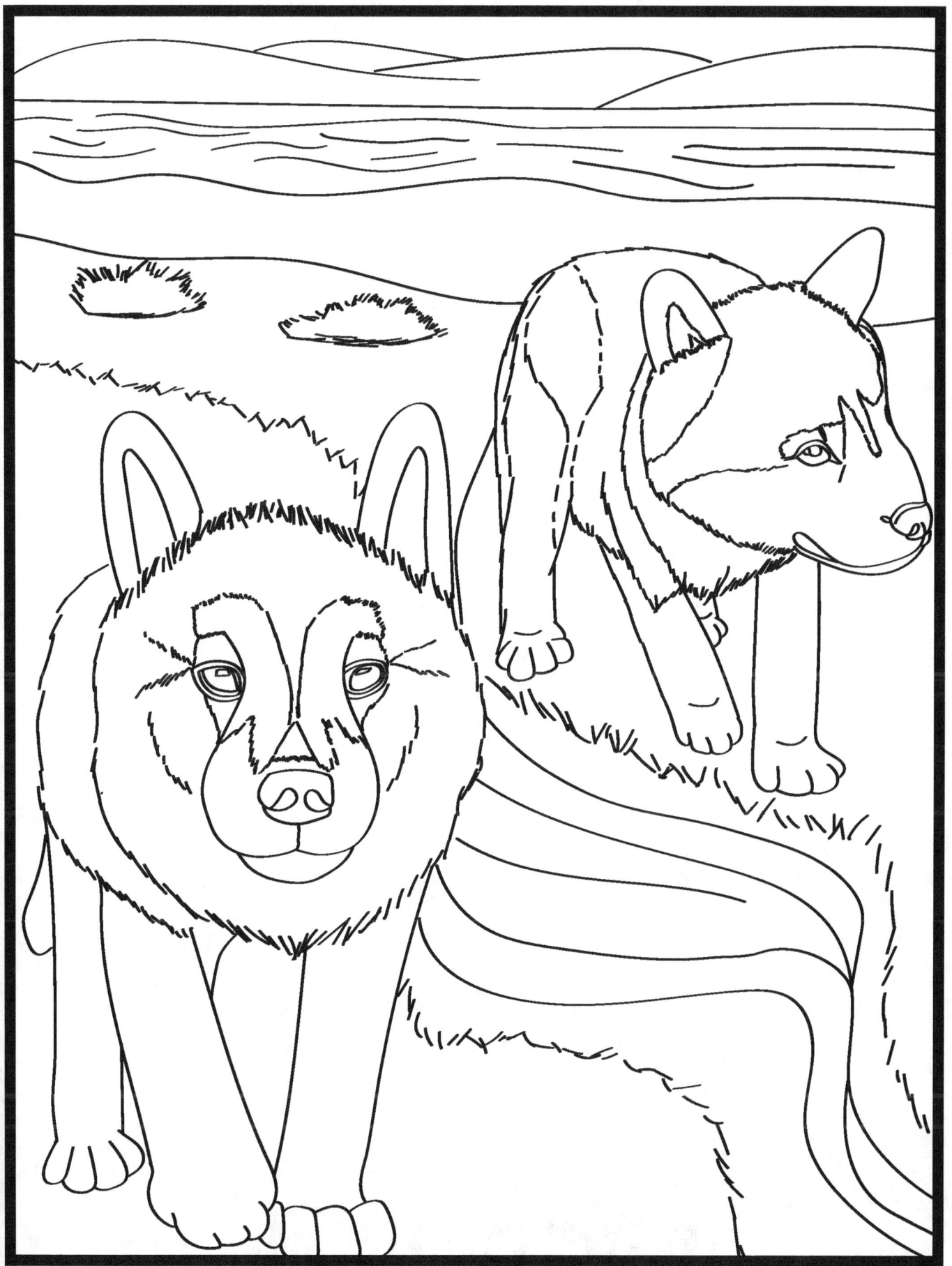

PLAYING ON THE BEACH

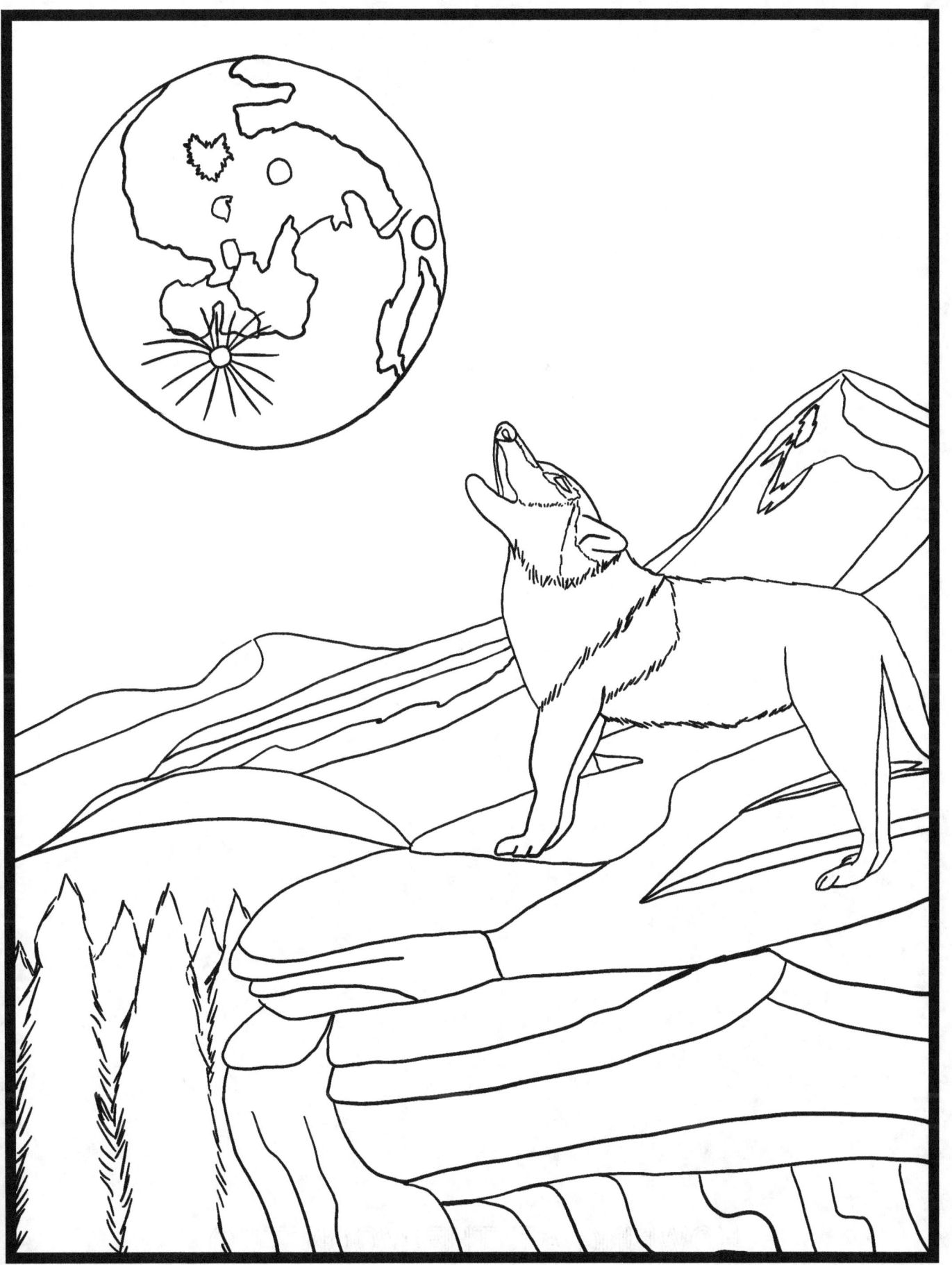

HOWLING AT THE MOON TOO

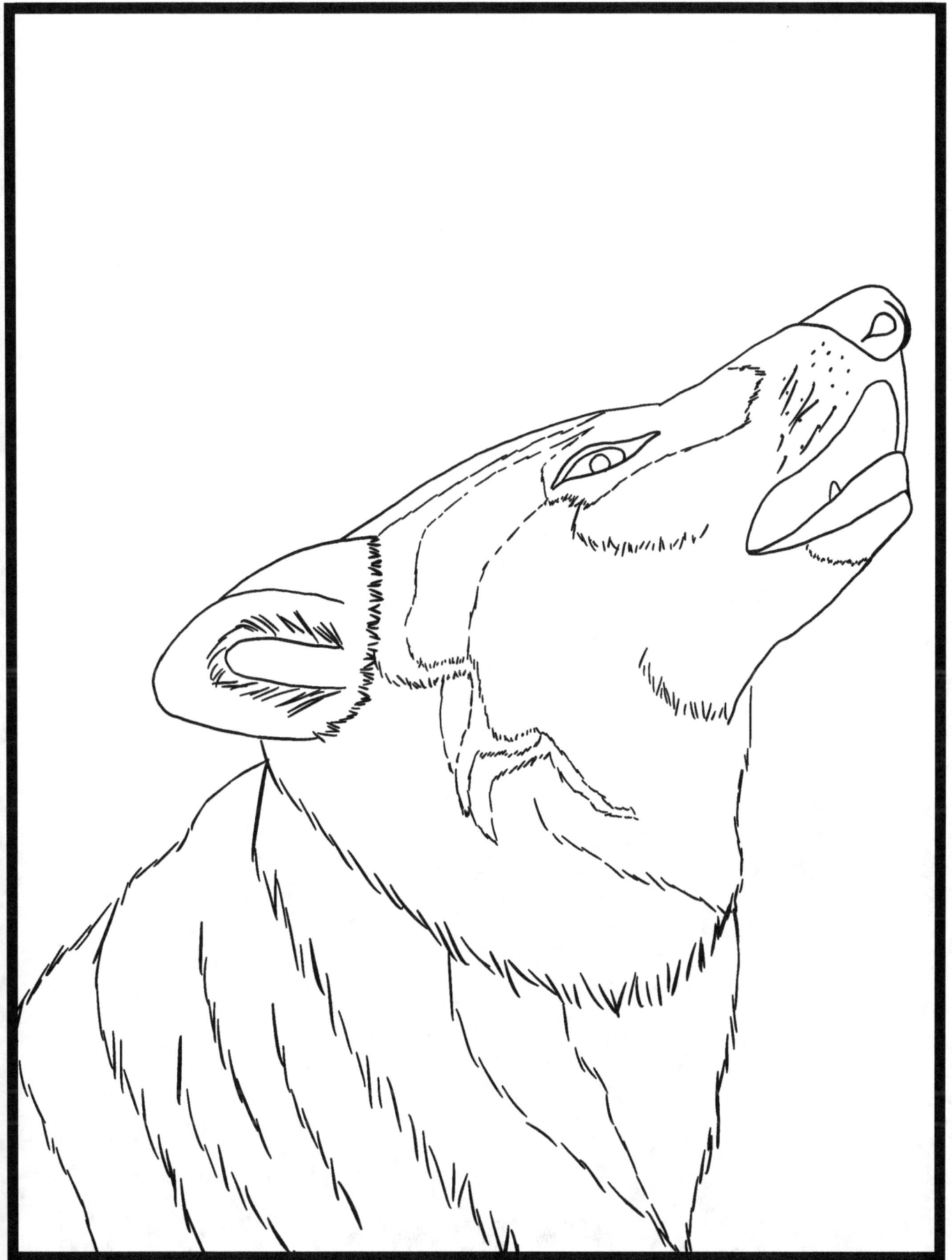

HOWLING BACK

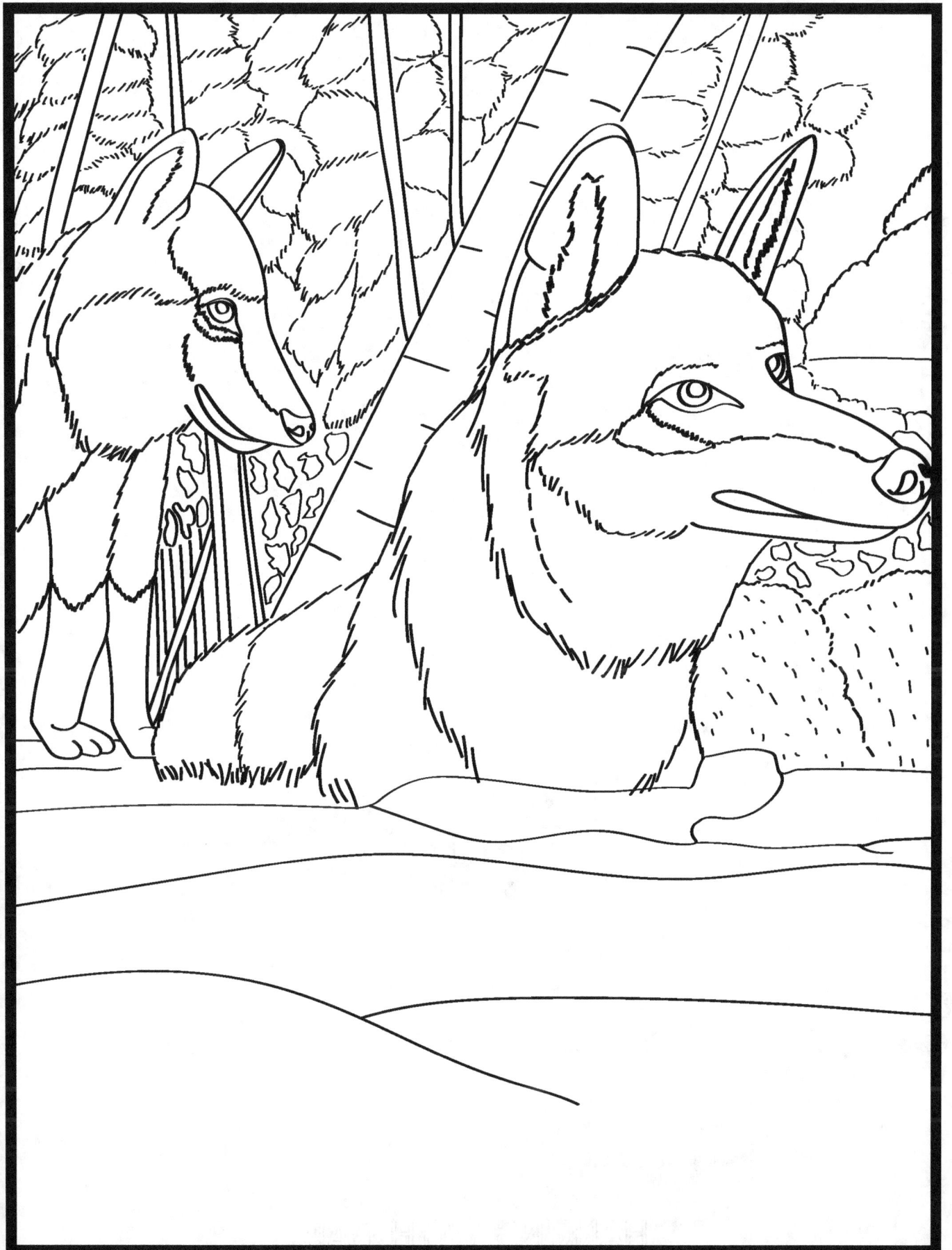

HANGING WITH DAD

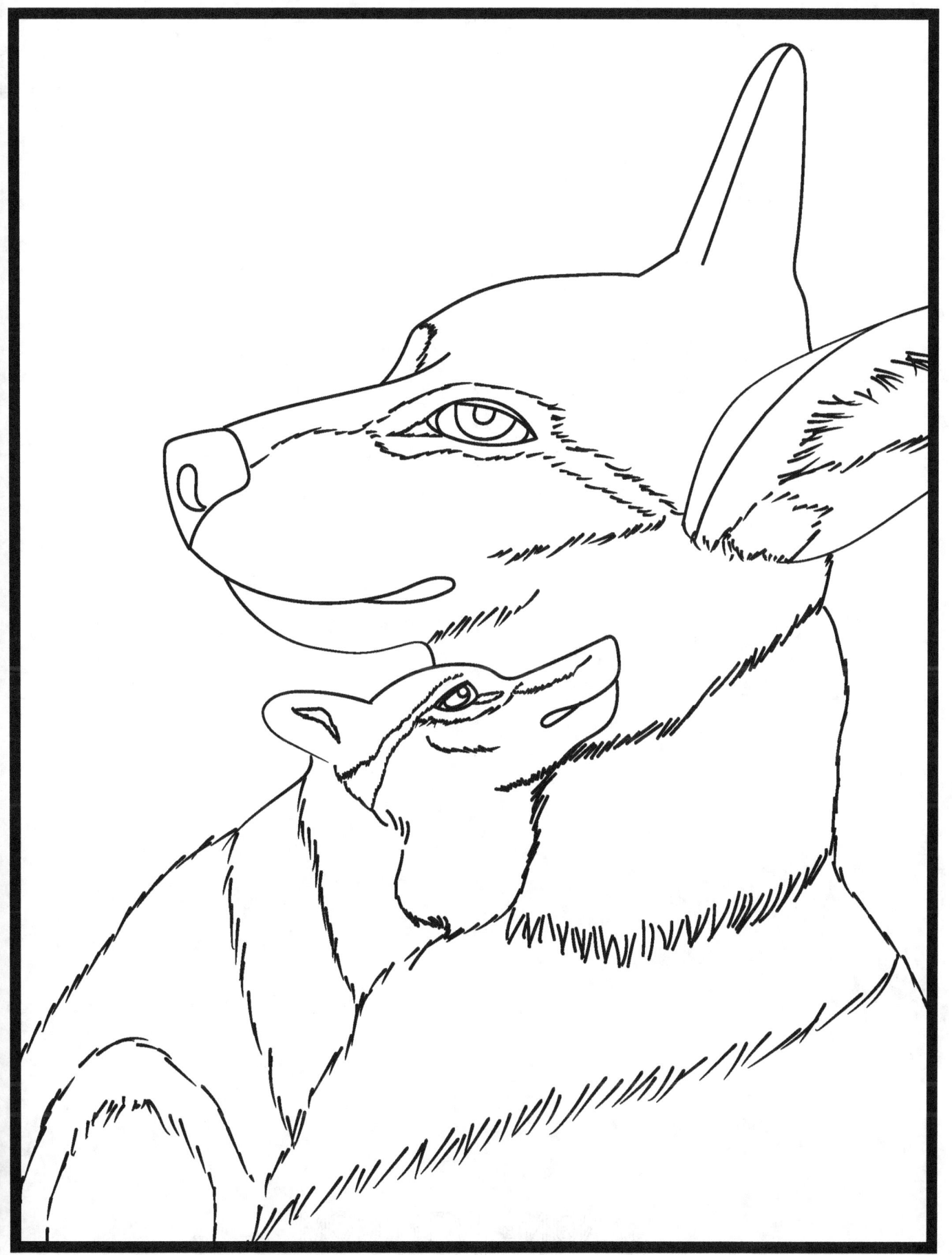

HANGING WITH MOM

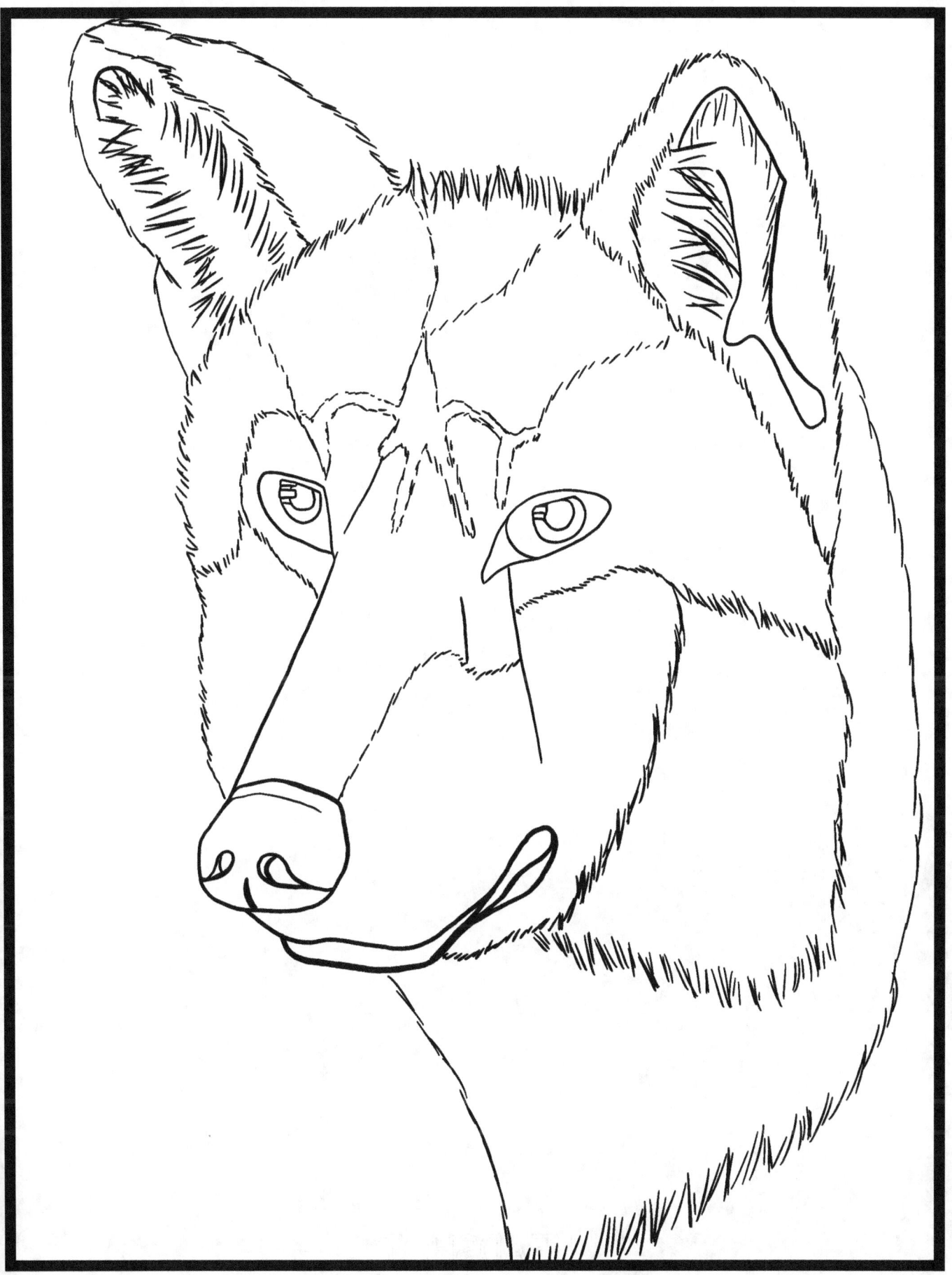

HEADSHOT

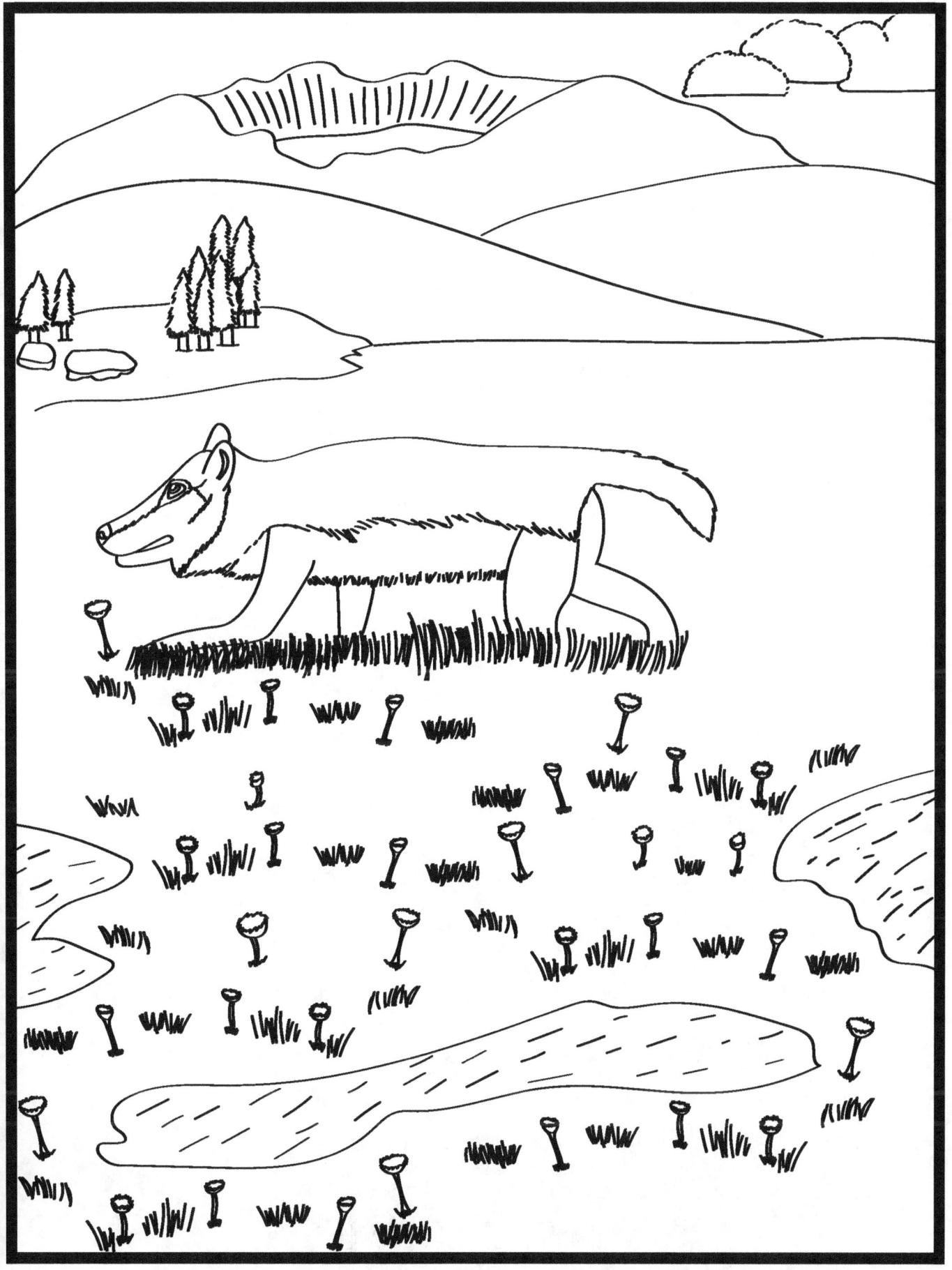

ON THE PROWL

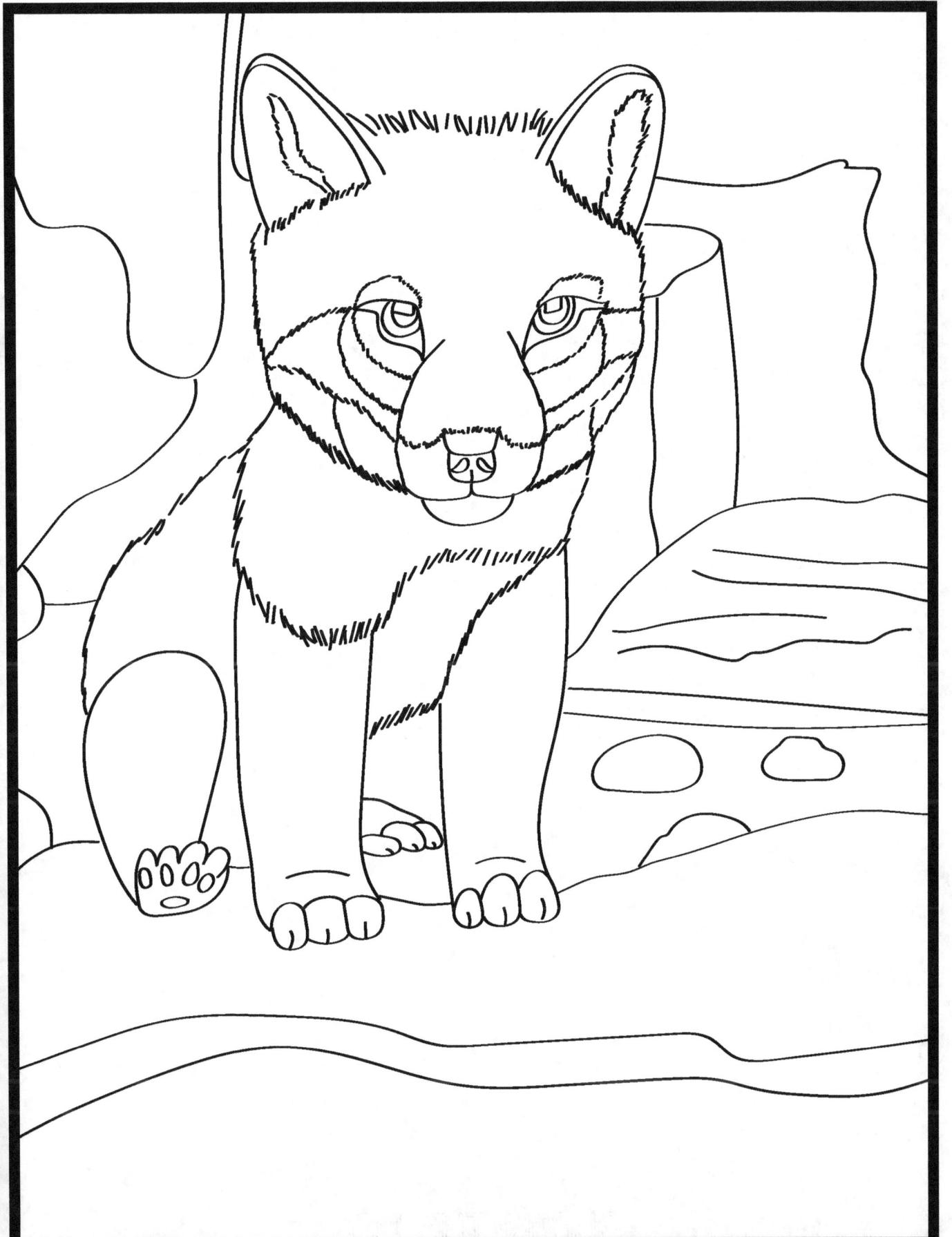

CUB IN THE DEN

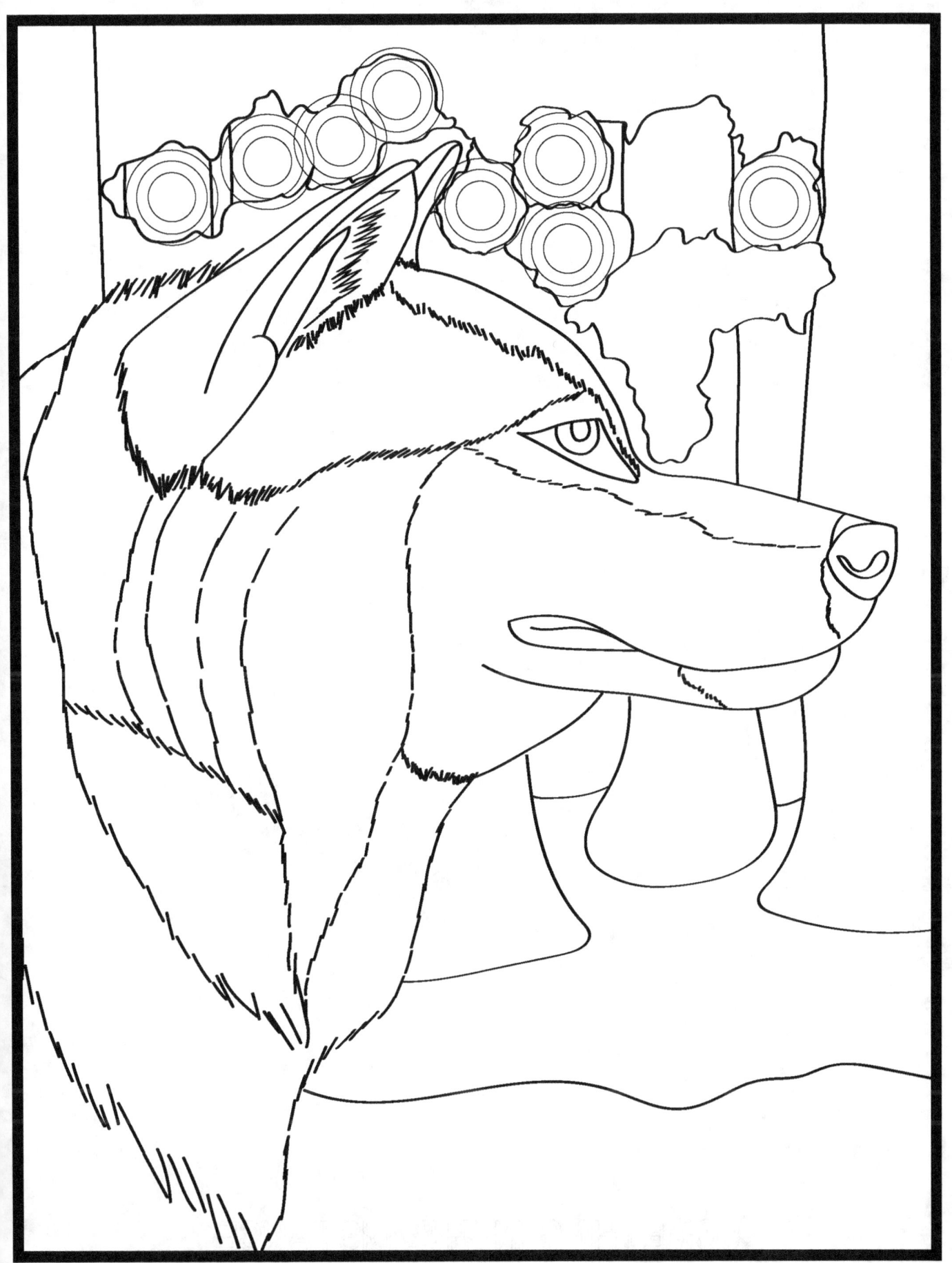

SOMETHING IN THE DISTANCE

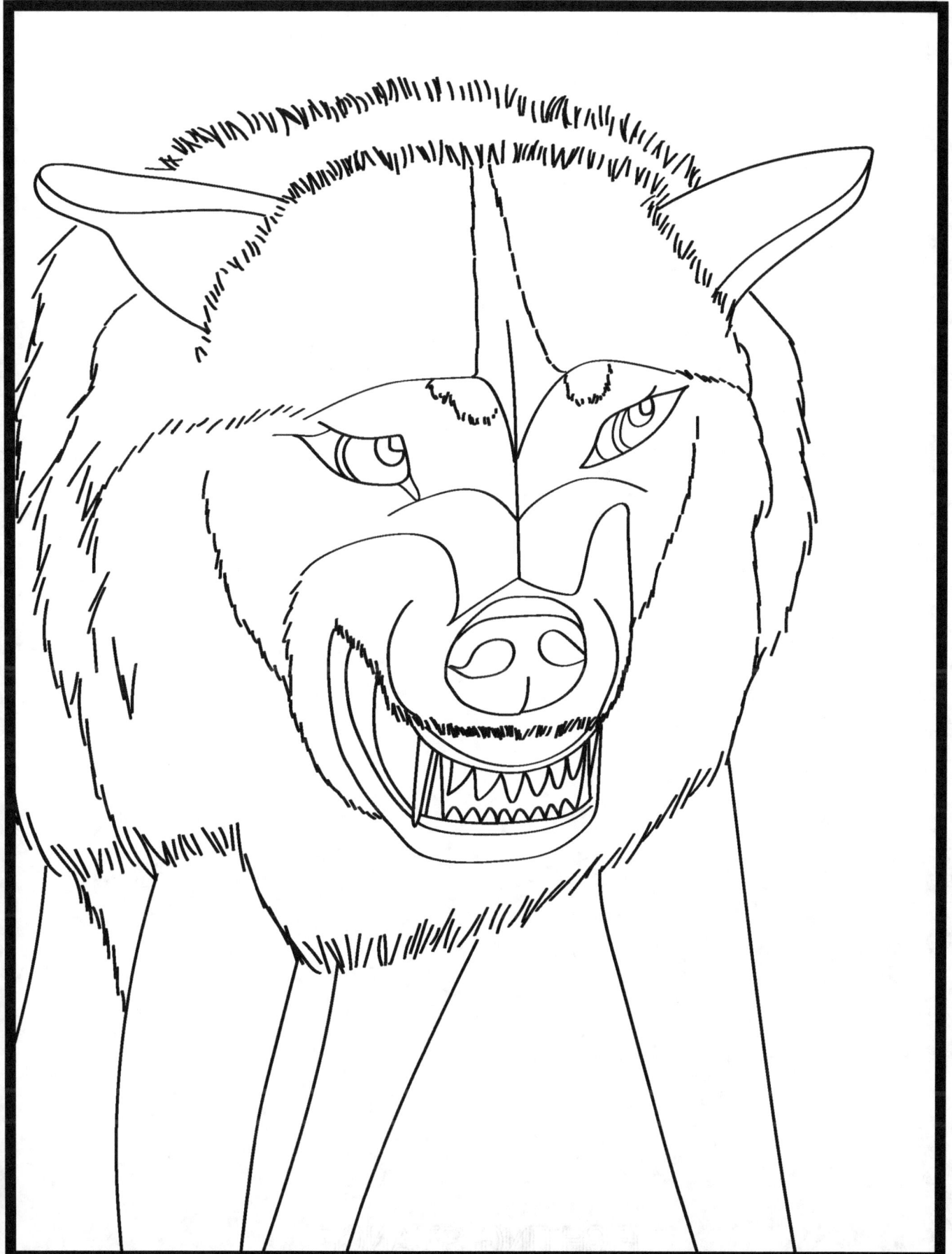

FIGHTING STANCE

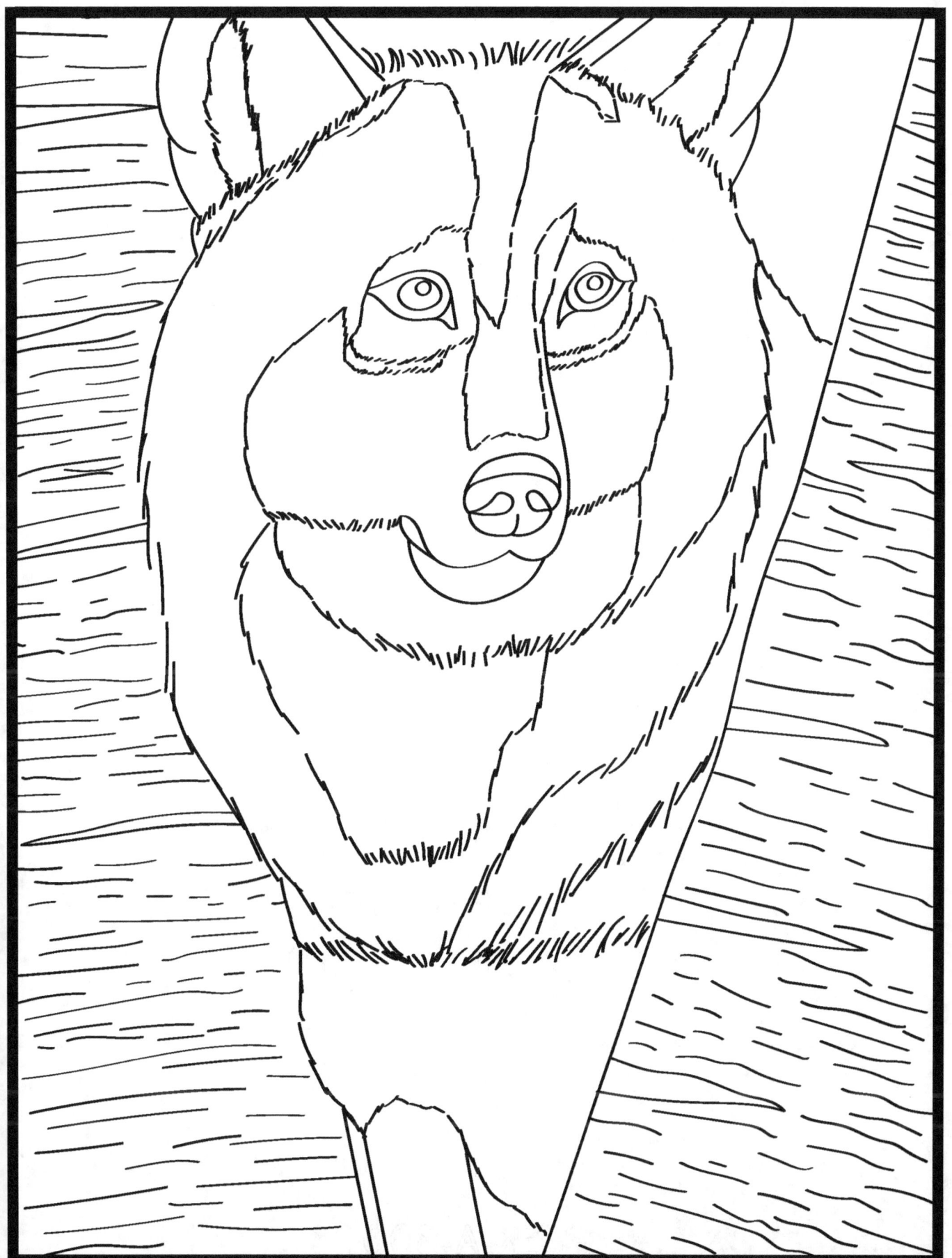

PEEK-A-BOO

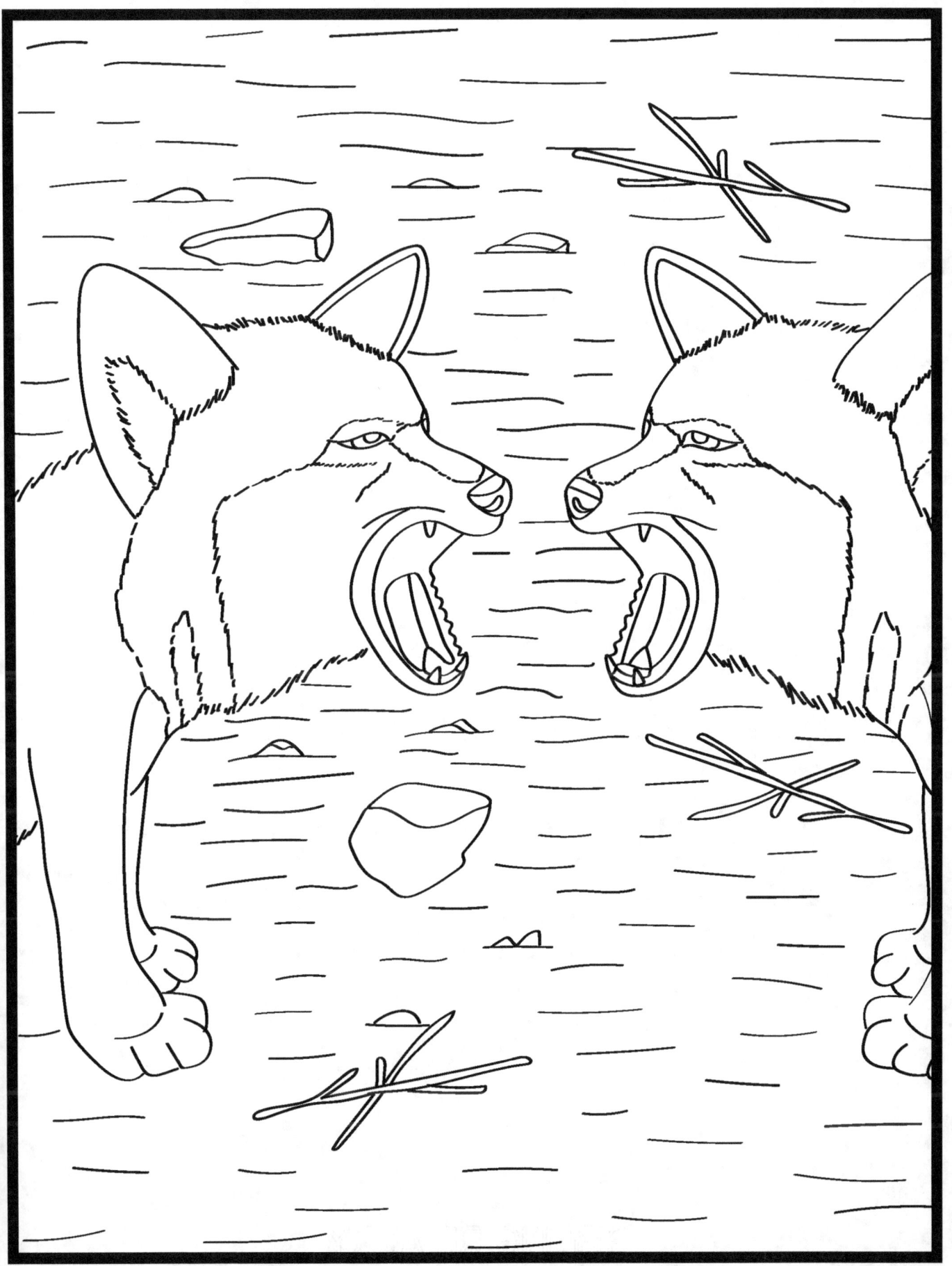

SIBLING RIVALRY

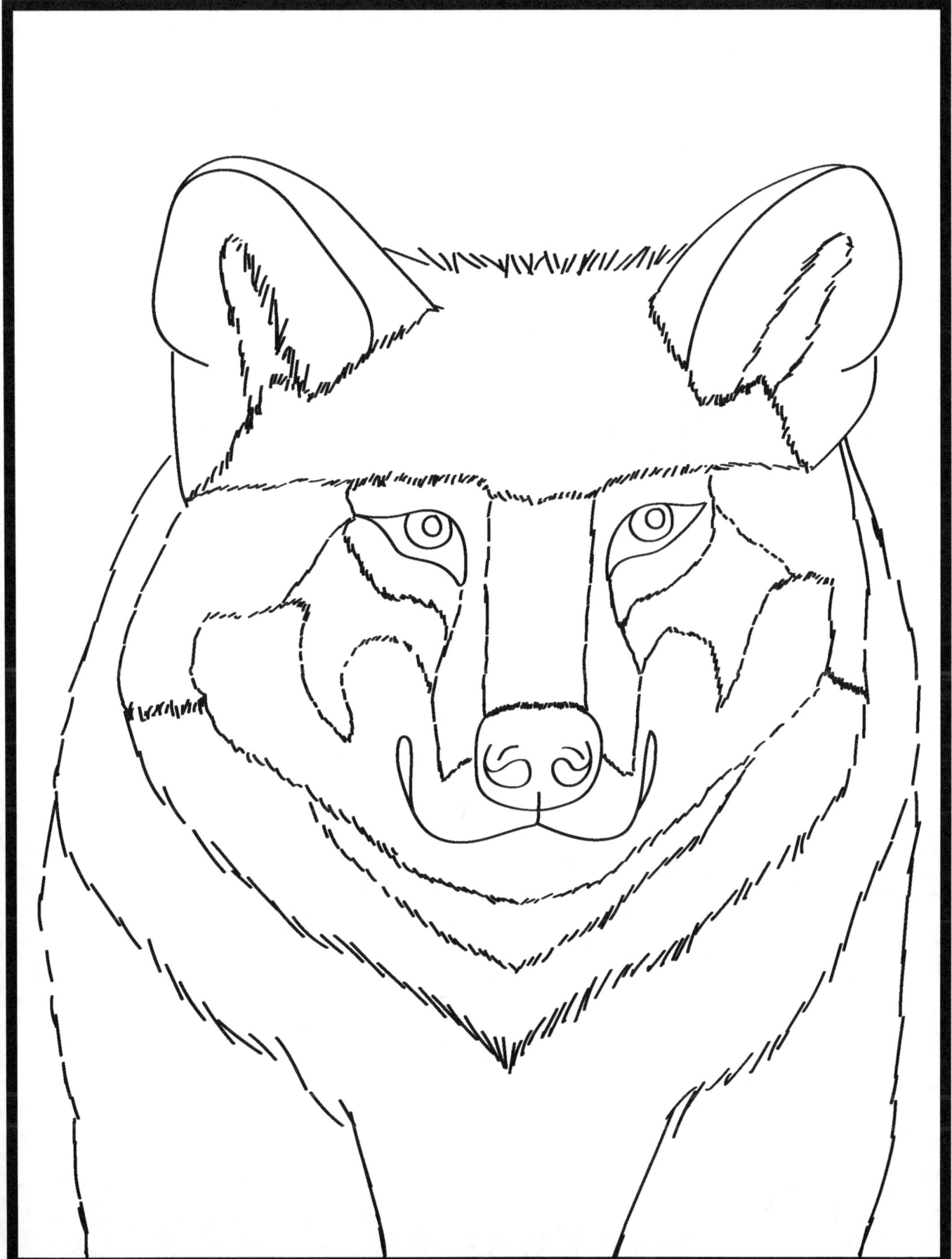

THE LONER

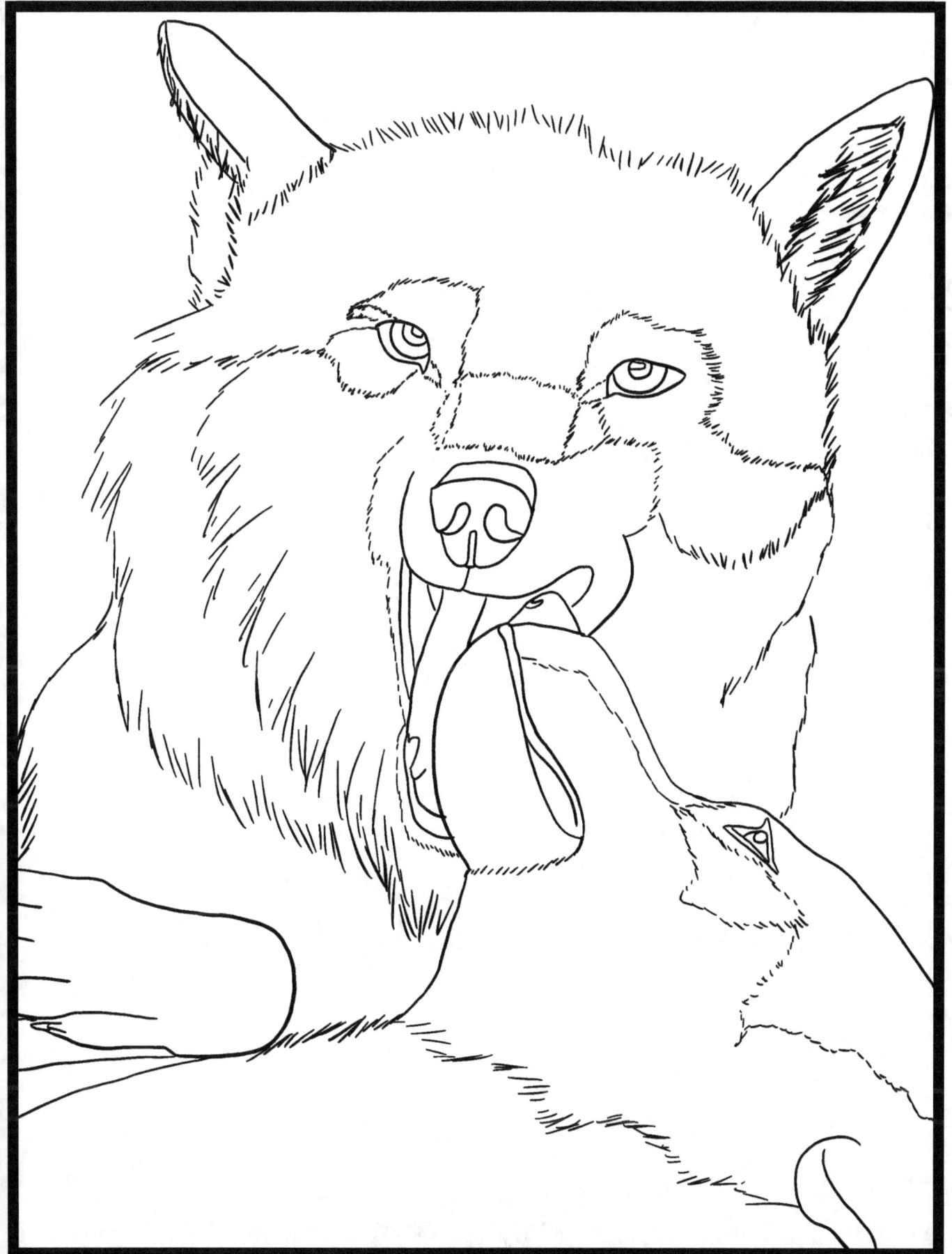

LOVE BIRDS

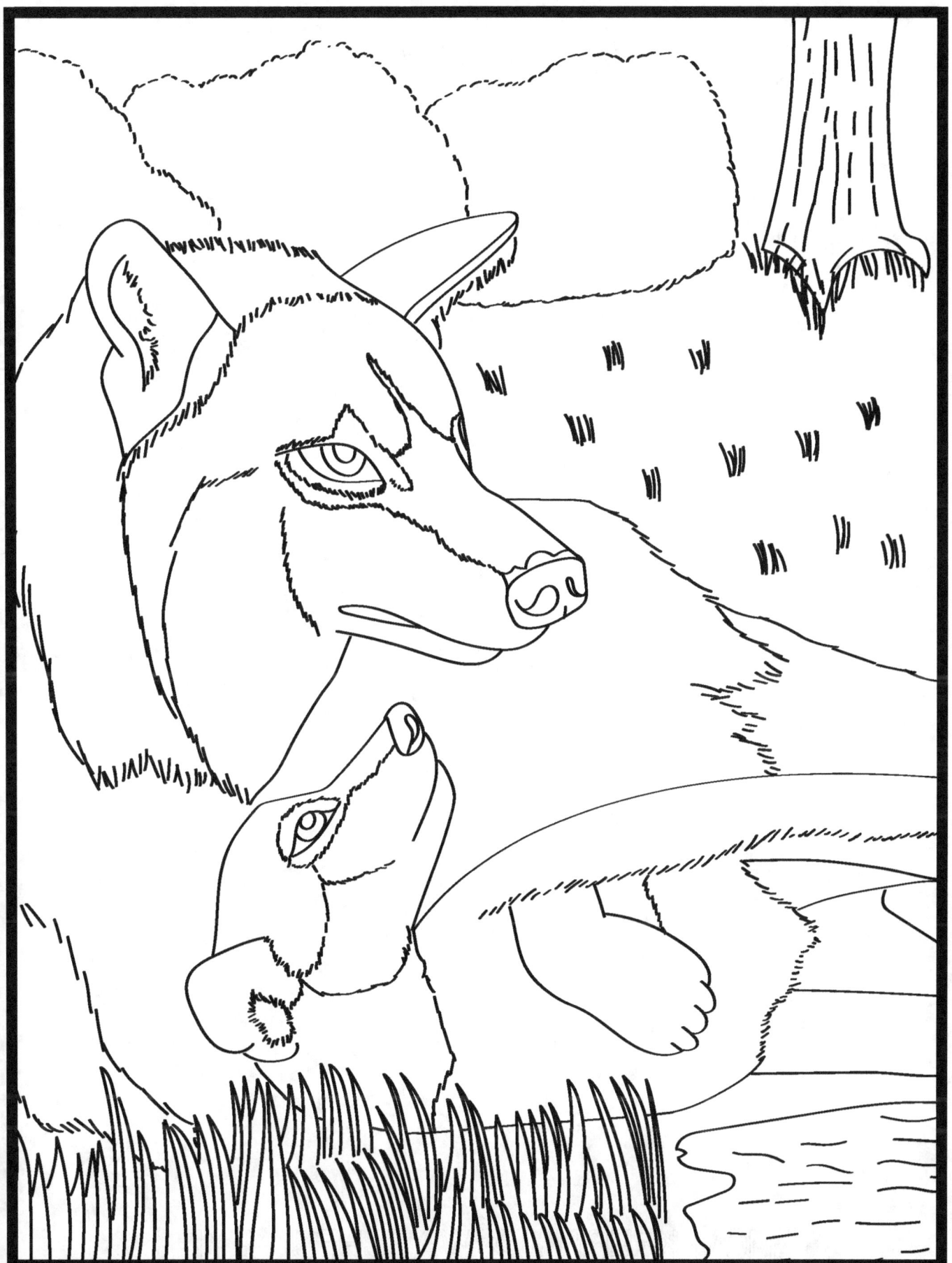

MOM KEEPING A WATCHFUL EYE

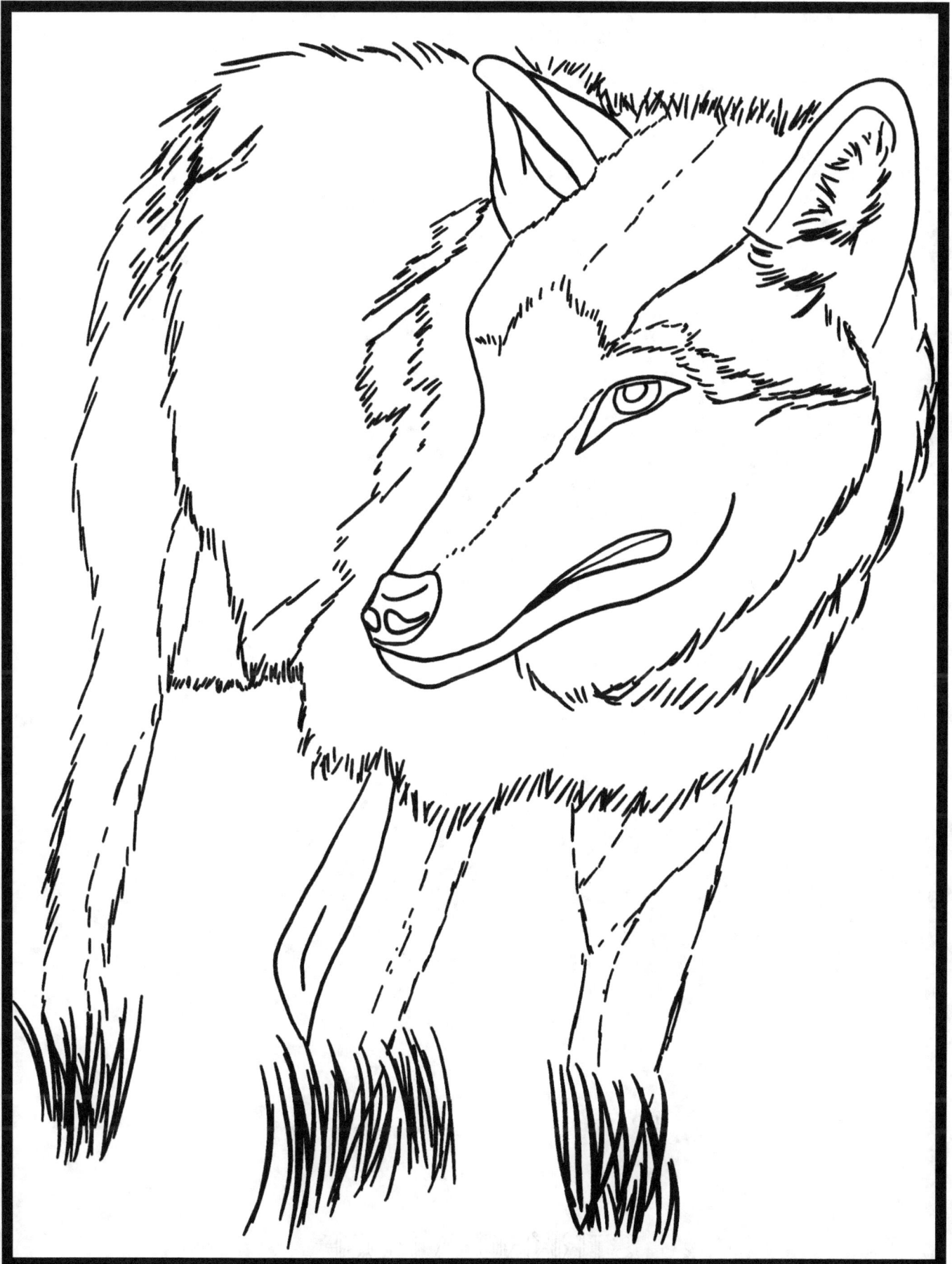

STRIKING A POSE

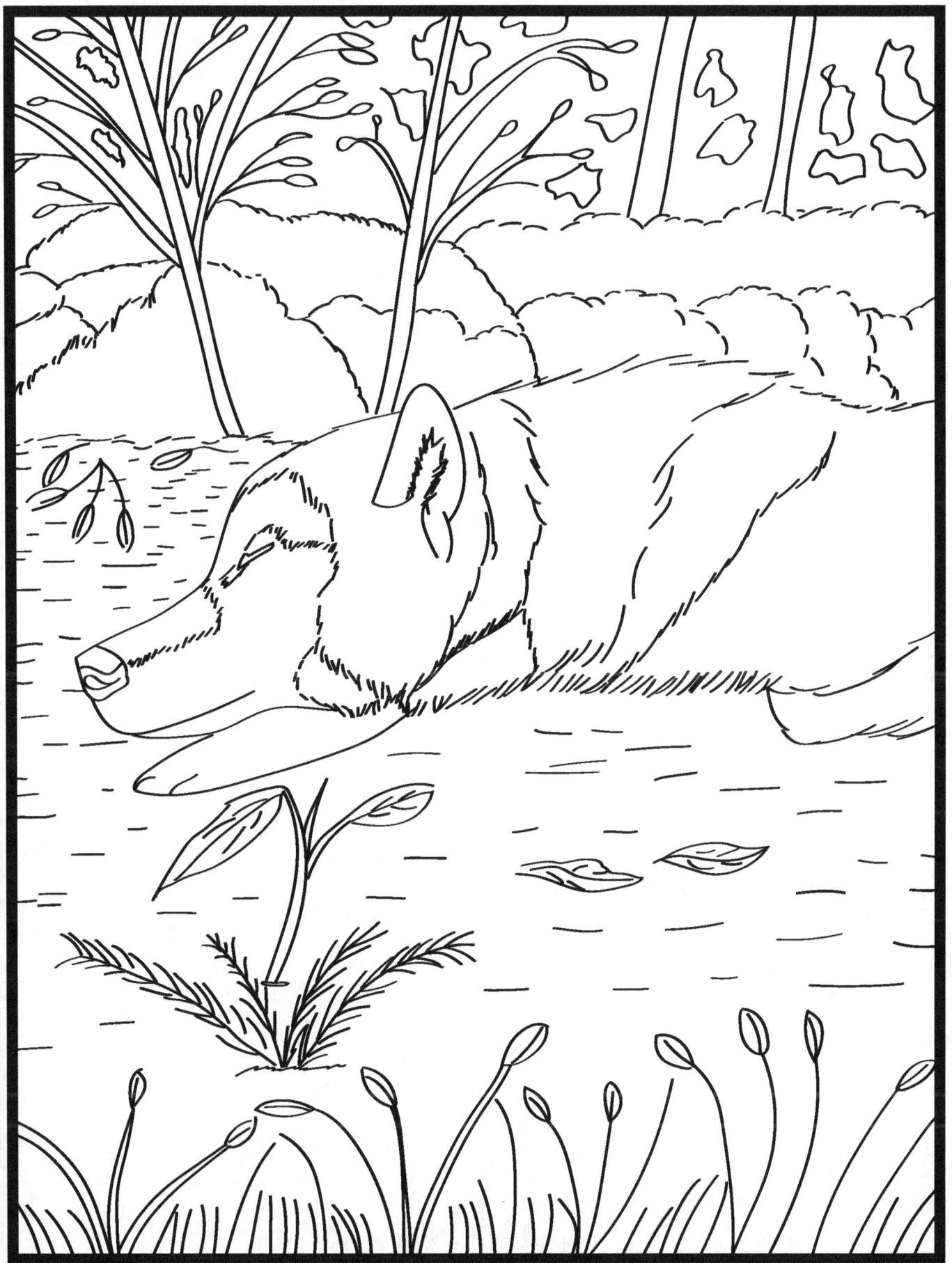

NAP TIME